ILLUMINATE THE FUTURE

ILLUMINATE *the* FUTURE

POPE FRANCIS IN CONVERSATION WITH RELIGIOUS SUPERIORS

COMPILED AND EDITED BY
Antonio Spadaro, SJ

Paulist Press
New York / Mahwah, NJ

Cover image by Elena Kichigina / Shutterstock.com
Cover and book design by Lynn Else

All material originally published in *La Civiltà Cattolica*. Copyright © 2014, 2015, 2017 by *La Civiltà Cattolica*
Portions have been published as *Illuminate il Futuro: Una conversazione raccontata da Antonio Spadaro* by Àncora Editrice, Milan. Copyright © 2015 Àncora S.r.l.
English translation copyright © 2022 by Paulist Press, Inc. Translated by Barry Hudock.

Library of Congress Cataloging-in-Publication Data
Names: Francis, Pope, 1936– interviewee. | Spadaro, Antonio, editor, compiler, interviewer. | Unione superiori generali, interviewer.
Title: Illuminate the future : Pope Francis in conversation with religious superiors / compiled and edited by Antonio Spadaro.
Other titles: Illuminate il futuro. English
Description: New York : Paulist Press, [2022] | "All material originally published in La Civiltà Cattolica. Copyright © 2014, 2015, 2017 by La Civiltà Cattolica. Portions have been published as Illuminate il Futuro: Una conversazione raccontata da Antonio Spadaro by Àncora. Editrice, Milan. Copyright © 2015 Àncora S.r.l." | Summary: "A distillation of the wisdom of Pope Francis on the subject of religious life, culled from meetings with religious superiors and other events and based on his years of experience as a Jesuit superior"— Provided by publisher.
Identifiers: LCCN 2021023908 (print) | LCCN 2021023909 (ebook) | ISBN 9780809155781 (paperback) | ISBN 9781587689772 (ebook)
Subjects: LCSH: Francis, Pope, 1936–Interviews. | Catholic Church—Doctrines. | Jesuits—Spiritual life. | Monastic and religious life—Papal documents. | Church renewal—Catholic Church. | Pastoral care. | Church and the world.
Classification: LCC BX1378.7 .F72613 2022 (print) | LCC BX1378.7 (ebook) | DDC 282.092—dc23
LC record available at https://lccn.loc.gov/2021023908
LC ebook record available at https://lccn.loc.gov/2021023909

ISBN 978-0-8091-5578-1 (paperback)
ISBN 978-1-58768-977-2 (e-book)

Published by Paulist Press
997 Macarthur Boulevard
Mahwah, New Jersey 07430
www.paulistpress.com

Printed and bound in the
United States of America

CONTENTS

v

CONTENTS

PREFACE

When Pope Francis granted an audience to the Union of Superiors General on November 29, 2013, at the conclusion of the organization's eighty-second general assembly, he made one thing clear: he did not want to make speeches and did not want to hear them. It was his intention to enter into the dynamics of the discussion of the superiors general, in order to reflect on important questions together and perhaps reach some conclusions. I was there to record the conversation. In trying to describe the experience, the best image I can offer is that of a spring of water: the dialogue that occurred flowed forth naturally, spontaneously, leaving all those present with a sense of having participated in an authentic and refreshing encounter. In this little book, the reader will find the story of that conversation.[1]

There was no expectation that the encounter would be summarized later in a document on religious life, but rather that it would be shared through an account that would retain its lively, conversational nature. For this reason, the following text is important. Originally published in *La Civiltà Cattolica*,[2] the journal I serve as editor, it was subsequently published in book form by the Italian publishing house Àncora to serve as a meditative text for the 2015 Year of Consecrated Life (plans for which were first formally announced at the very November 2013 general assembly we are talking about here), and it is now presented here for the English-language audience by Paulist Press.

But this encounter was certainly not the first time that Pope Francis had addressed the topic of religious life. For this reason, my account of the meeting with the superiors general is followed by a careful look at several important precedents. We'll begin with the intervention that Bishop Jorge Mario Bergoglio, then auxiliary bishop of Buenos Aires, offered during the 1994 meeting of the Synod of Bishops on the topic of the consecrated life and its role in the church and in the world. After that, we'll look at some reflections that Bergoglio has offered over time, from the time he served as provincial of the Jesuits of Argentina up to and including his more recent comments as pope. In following this path, we will identify eight principal challenges that he sees facing consecrated religious life today. These include recognizing ourselves as sinners saved by grace, discernment that seeks and finds God in all things, open-ended thinking, prophecy, generativity, fraternity, mission, and finally, consolation.

From these brushstrokes emerges the portrait of a complex and multifaceted life, but one that is worth living.

Antonio Spadaro, SJ
Editor-in-Chief, *La Civiltà Cattolica*

A CONVERSATION WITH RELIGIOUS SUPERIORS, NOVEMBER 29, 2013

INTRODUCTION—9:25 A.M., THE VATICAN SYNOD HALL

When Pope Francis speaks "off the cuff" or engages in a dialogue, his speech has a distinctive rhythm and flow that must be followed carefully because it reflects an active engagement with those with whom he is talking. Anyone who seeks to report it must pay attention not only to his words, but also to the relational dynamic that emerges. This was the case for the Holy Father's conversation with the members of the Union of Superiors General (USG) of the male religious orders and congregations, on November 29, 2013—just over eight months into his pontificate.[1]

Sitting among them, I paid attention to the dialogue. Here I will try to express the richness of its content, preserving the lively and spontaneous nature of the exchange, which lasted for three hours. Halfway through, there was a half-hour break, during which the pope took the opportunity to personally greet each of the superiors general, even enjoying a *maté*—the traditional South American caffeine-rich drink—with them in a relaxed atmosphere.

In truth, the superiors had only requested a brief audience with the pope, to conclude their eighty-second general assembly. But the pontiff had other plans. He dedicated an entire morning to the event. But he chose not to give any speech and not to listen to previously prepared reports or remarks. Instead, he asked for a frank and free conversation with those present, an exchange of questions and answers.

At 9:25 a.m., the arrival of the photographers announced his imminent entry into the Vatican's Synod Hall, where about 120 superiors awaited him.

RELIGIOUS WOMEN AND MEN: SINNERS AND PROPHETS

Greeted by applause, the Holy Father sat down at 9:30 sharp, looked at his watch, and congratulated himself on his "Swiss punctuality," provoking laughter in the hall. The pope greeted Br. Mauro Jöhri, the minister general of the order of Friars Minor Capuchin, who had just been elected vice president of the USG.

After brief greetings by Fr. Adolfo Nicolás, president of the USG and superior general of the Jesuits, and by Fr. David Glenday, the USG general secretary and a Comboni Missionary, Pope Francis offered his thanks for the invitation and then listened as a first group of questions was offered to him.

The first questions from those present were about the identity and mission of religious: "What do you expect from people engaged in consecrated life? What are you asking? If you were in our place, how would you respond to the call you have issued to go to the peripheries, to live the Gospel *sine glossa*, prophetically? What would you feel called to do? Where should the emphasis be placed today? What should be the priorities?"

Pope Francis began by noting that he too is a consecrated religious and that he therefore understands from experience the concerns that the men were raising.[2] The last pope from a religious order was the Camaldolese monk Gregory XVI (1765–1846), elected in 1831. Francis then recalled a comment made by Pope Benedict XVI in 2007:

> He said the church grows by witness, not by proselytism.[3] The witness that can truly attract is one that expresses attitudes that are uncommon today: generosity, detachment, sacrifice, self-forgetfulness in order to take care of others.

3

That is the witness, the "martyrdom" of religious life. It is a "wake-up call" for people. Religious, by the way they live, cause people to say, "What is going on? These people have something to say to me! These people have their eyes fixed on a different horizon!" And so religious life must nourish the growth of the church through this way of attraction.

Therefore, Francis said,

The church must be attractive. Wake up the world! Be witnesses of a different way of doing things, of acting, of living! It is possible to live differently in this world. We are talking about an eschatological gaze, about the values of the kingdom made incarnate here on this earth. It is about leaving everything to follow the Lord. No, I don't mean it's about religious living "radically." The radicalism of the Gospel is not only for religious; it is required of all. But religious follow the Lord in a special way, in a prophetic way. I expect this witness from you. Religious must be men and women who can wake up the world.

Pope Francis developed and deepened the ideas he was expressing. He continued,

You must be authentic witnesses of a different way of acting and living. But it is difficult for everything in life to be clear, precise, and neatly organized. Life is complex; it includes both grace and sin. Someone who doesn't sin isn't human. We all make mistakes, and we must recognize our weakness. A religious who recognizes himself as weak and sinful does not contradict the witness he is called to give, but rather strengthens it, and this is good for everyone. What I expect, therefore, is that you give witness. I desire this special witness from religious.

AVOIDING FUNDAMENTALISM, ILLUMINATING THE FUTURE

Continuing with his responses to the initial questions, Pope Francis touched upon one of the key points of his thought:

I am convinced of this: the great changes in history took place when reality was viewed not from the center, but from the periphery. It is a hermeneutical question; reality is fully understood only if we look at it from the periphery, and not from a center equidistant from everything. To truly understand reality, we must move away from the central position of calm and tranquility and move to the periphery. Looking from the periphery helps one to see and understand better, to form a more accurate analysis of reality, avoiding centralism and ideological approaches.

Therefore, the pope said,

> It is not necessary to be in the center of a sphere.
> To understand, we have to "disconnect," to look
> at reality from different points of view.[4] We have
> to get used to thinking. I often refer to a letter
> of Fr. Pedro Arrupe, who was superior general
> of the Society of Jesus. It was a letter addressed
> to the Centers for Social Research and Action.
> In this letter, Fr. Arrupe spoke of poverty, and
> he said that it was necessary to spend real time
> in contact with the poor. For me this is really
> important: you have to know reality from expe-
> rience, take the time to go to the peripheries to
> really get to know the reality and people's expe-
> riences. If this doesn't happen, then there is the
> risk that we become abstract ideologues or fun-
> damentalists, and this is not healthy.[5]

The pope then offered the concrete example of ministry to young people:

> Those who work with young people cannot
> simply talk as though everything is orderly and
> structured, like a treatise, because this approach
> is lost on young people. We need a new lan-
> guage, a new way of saying things. Today God
> asks us this: to leave our protective nest and to
> go forth. Even those who live their consecration
> in the cloister are called to live this interior ten-
> sion in prayer for the spread of the Gospel. The

fulfillment of the Gospel mandate to "go into all the world and proclaim the good news to the whole creation" (Mark 16:15) can be achieved through this hermeneutical key of moving to the existential and geographical peripheries. It is the most concrete way of imitating Jesus, who went to all the peripheries. Jesus went toward everyone, absolutely everyone. I would not feel at all uneasy going to the periphery. You shouldn't feel uncomfortable reaching out to anyone.

To the question of what the priority of consecrated life ought to be, the pope answered,

The prophecy of the kingdom, which is non-negotiable. The emphasis must fall on being prophets and not on playing at being one. Of course, the devil presents his temptations to us, and this is one of them: playing at being prophets, assuming their attitudes, without actually being one. But you can't pretend in these things. I myself have seen some very sad things in this regard. No—consecrated religious are men and women who illuminate the future.

In his 2013 interview with *La Civiltà Cattolica* and several Jesuit journals, Pope Francis had clearly stated that religious are called to a prophetic life. It is their distinctive vocation

to be prophets in particular by demonstrating how Jesus lived on this earth, and to proclaim how the kingdom of God will be in its perfection. A religious must never give up prophecy....Let us think about what so many great saints, monks and religious men and women have done, from St. Anthony the Abbot onward. Being prophets may sometimes imply making waves. I do not know how to put it....Prophecy makes noise, uproar, some say "a mess." But in reality, the charism of religious people is like yeast: prophecy announces the spirit of the Gospel.[6]

So, how can we be prophets living our own particular religious charisms? For Pope Francis, it is necessary "to strengthen what is institutional in consecrated life and not to confuse the religious order with its apostolic work. The former remains, the latter passes." The pope explained, "The charism remains, it is strong; the work passes. Sometimes the order and its ministry are confused. The order is creative; it is always looking for new paths. So even the peripheries change, and one can always make a different list."

"A CHARISM IS NOT A BOTTLE OF DISTILLED WATER"

At this point, the questions posed to the pope turned to the theme of vocations. A profound change is taking place today in the human geography of the church and therefore also of religious orders. Vocations in Africa and Asia, which account for the majority of the total number, are growing. All this poses serious challenges: the inculturation of the charism, vocational discernment and the selection of candidates, the challenge of interreligious dialogue, the need for more equitable representation in the governing bodies of the orders and, more generally, in the structure of the church. The superiors asked the pope for some guidance in this situation.

Pope Francis said he understands that the geography of consecrated life has changed a great deal and that

> people of all cultures have the capacity to be called by the Lord, who is free to arouse more vocations in one region or another. What does the Lord want with the vocations he sends us from the younger churches? I don't know. But I ask myself the question. We have to ask ourselves. The Lord's will is somewhere in all of this. There are churches that are bearing new fruit. Maybe they weren't very fruitful at one time, but now they are. This naturally obliges us to rethink the inculturation of the charism. The charism is one, but, as Saint Ignatius said, it must be lived according to places, times, and people.
>
> A charism is not a bottle of distilled water. It must be lived dynamically, understood in new ways according to the culture it's in.
>
> But, one might object, that introduces a risk of making mistakes. It's risky. Of course, of course.

We will always make mistakes, there is no doubt. But this shouldn't stop us, because that brings a risk of bigger mistakes. In fact, we must always ask for forgiveness and look with great shame at the apostolic failures that have occurred because of a lack of courage. We might think, for example, of Matteo Ricci's pioneering ideas that were ignored in his time.[7]

Francis continued,

I'm not talking simply about a folkloristic adaptation to customs. It's a question of mentality, of ways of thinking. For example, there are peoples who think more concretely than abstractly or who at least have a type of abstraction different than in the West. I myself experienced this difference as provincial of the Jesuits in Argentina. I remember how much effort we made at dialogue, even about the simple things of daily life, with a Jesuit brother who came from the area of the Guarani people, who had developed a very concrete way of thinking. We must live with courage and face these challenges even on important issues.

In short, we can't form a person as a religious without taking into consideration his or her life, experience, mentality, and cultural context. This is the way. This is what the great missionary religious have done. I am reminded of the extraordinary adventures of the Spanish Jesuit

Segundo Llorente, a tenacious and contemplative missionary in Alaska, who learned not only the language but also the concrete way of thinking of the people he served.[8]

Inculturating the charism is fundamental, and this never means relativizing it. We can't make the charism rigid or uniform. When we standardize our cultures, then we kill the charism.

The pontiff concluded by insisting on the need "to introduce into the central leadership of the orders people of various cultures, who express different ways of living the charism."

Pope Francis is certainly aware of the risks related to "vocational recruitment" in the younger churches. Among other things, he recalled that in 1994, during the meeting of the Synod of Bishops on the theme of consecrated life and its mission, the Filipino bishops denounced the "novice trade," that is, the massive arrival of foreign orders opening houses in the Philippines for the purpose of recruiting vocations that would quickly be transplanted to Europe. "We need to keep our eyes open to these situations," the pope said.

He then turned to the topic of the vocation of brothers and, more generally, of religious who are not priests. He expressed his concern that we have not yet developed an adequate understanding of this particular vocation. He mentioned an official document on the topic that had been prepared in Rome but was never published; he suggested that perhaps it should be taken up again in order to prompt a more adequate reflection on the topic. At this point, the pope turned to Cardinal João Braz de Aviz, prefect of the Congregation for Institutes of Consecrated Life and Societies of Apostolic Life, and to that congregation's secretary, Archbishop José Rodríguez Carballo, who were present at the assembly, and invited them to consider the matter. He concluded, "I don't believe at all that the crisis of the vocation of nonordained religious is a sign of the times that says this vocation is over. Rather, we have to understand what God is asking of us."

Then, responding to a question about religious brothers as superiors in clerical orders, the pope replied that it is a canonical issue that should be addressed at that level.

"FORMATION IS A WORK OF ART, NOT OF LAW ENFORCEMENT"

Pope Francis then received some questions on the subject of formation. He replied, explaining his own priorities:

The formation of candidates is fundamental. There are four pillars of formation: spiritual, intellectual, communal, and apostolic. The ghost that we have to fight against is the image of religious life as an escape or a protection from a difficult and complex world "out there." The four pillars must be integrated from the very beginning of the novitiate; they can't be followed in sequence. There must be an interaction.

The pope is aware of the fact that the challenge of formation today is not easy. He said,

> Today's culture is much richer and more conflictual than what we experienced in our time, years ago. Our culture was simpler and more orderly. Today, inculturation requires a different attitude. For example, problems can't be solved simply by prohibiting young religious from doing this or that. We need a lot of dialogue, a lot of discussion. In some houses of formation, young people avoid problems by gritting their teeth, trying not to make obvious mistakes. They stick to the rules and smile a lot, awaiting the day they will one day be told, "Okay, your formation is complete." This is hypocrisy that results from clericalism, which is one of the most terrible evils. I said this to the bishops of the Latin American episcopal conference this summer in Rio de Janeiro, that this tendency toward clericalism in houses of formation and seminaries must be overcome. I summarize it in a piece of advice I once received as a young man: "If you want to move forward, think clearly and speak obscurely." It was a clear invitation to hypocrisy. It must be avoided at all costs.

In Rio de Janeiro, in fact, at the 2013 World Youth Day celebrations, the pope identified clericalism as one of the causes of the "lack of maturity and Christian freedom" of the people of God.[9]

Therefore, the pope told the superiors,

> If the seminary is too large, it should be divided into smaller communities so that formators are truly capable of accompanying people. The dialogue must be serious, fearless, sincere. And we must keep in mind that the language of young people in formation today is different from that of those who preceded them; we are experiencing a change of era. Formation is a work of art, not of law enforcement. We have to form their hearts. Otherwise we create little monsters. And then these little monsters form the people of God. This really gives me goosebumps.

The pope then insisted that formation must be oriented not only to personal growth, but to its ultimate purpose: the people of God. In forming religious, formation staff must think of the people they will one day serve. The pope said,

> We must always think of the faithful, the faithful people of God. We have to form people who are witnesses of the resurrection of Jesus. The formator must remember that the person in formation will be called to care for the people of God. We must always think of the people of God, as one of them. Let us recall those religious who have hearts as acidic as vinegar: they are not

made for the people. In short, we must not form administrators or managers, but fathers, brothers, companions on the journey.

Finally, Pope Francis sought to highlight a further risk:

> If a young person who has been asked to leave a religious order due to formation problems and for serious reasons is then accepted into a seminary, this is another big issue. I'm not talking about people who recognize that they are sinners; we are all sinners, but not all of us are corrupt. Sinners can be accepted, but not people who are corrupt.

And here the pope recalled the great resolve of Pope Benedict XVI in dealing with cases of abuse. "It must serve as an example for us," he said, "to have the courage to take personal formation as a serious challenge, always bearing in mind the people of God."

LIVING FRATERNITY BY RESOLVING CONFLICTS

The 2012 meeting of the Synod of Bishops on the new evangelization called on religious women and men to be witnesses of the humanizing power of the Gospel through their fraternal life. Taking a cue from this appeal, some questions were addressed to the pope about the fraternal life of religious: "How do we fulfill both the commitment to mission and the commitment to community life? How do we resist the pull toward individualism? How do we deal effectively with brothers in difficulty or who create conflicts? How do we combine justice and mercy in response to difficult cases?"

Pope Francis noted that the previous day he had received a visit from the prior of Taizé, Br. Alois. He said,

> In Taizé, there are monks who are Catholic, Calvinist, Lutheran...all truly live a life of fraternity. They are an impressive, attractive force for young people. Fraternity has an enormous power to call people together. The threats to fraternity, on the other hand, have a destructive force. The temptation against fraternity is what most impedes a journey in consecrated life. The individualistic tendency is basically a way of corroding fraternity. Saint John Berchmans[10] said that his greatest penance was community life. Sometimes it is difficult to live fraternity, but one who does not live it is not fruitful. Work, even of an "apostolic" kind, can become an escape from fraternal life. If a person fails to live fraternity, he cannot live the religious life.
>
> Religious fraternity, in all its possible variations, is an experience of love that goes beyond conflicts. Community conflicts are inevitable; in

a certain sense, they *must* exist if the community truly lives sincere and honest relationships. That's life. Imagining a community without brothers who sometimes have difficulties makes no sense, and it is not good. If there is no conflict in a community, it means something is missing. Reality tells us that there's conflict in all families and in all human groups. And conflict must be faced; it can't be ignored. If it is covered up, it creates pressure and then explodes. A life without conflict is not real life.

The stakes are high. We know that one of Pope Francis's fundamental principles is that "unity prevails over conflict."[11] His words to religious should be read in the light of sections 226–30 of *Evangelii Gaudium*, where he calls people to "face conflict head on, to resolve it, and to make it a link in the chain of a new process."[12] We must remember that for Bergoglio, personal fulfillment is never an exclusively individual undertaking; it is a collective and communal one.[13] In this sense, conflict can, and indeed must, evolve in a process of maturation.

In any case, conflict must be addressed with accompaniment. Francis said,

We can never behave like the priest or the Levite in the parable of the Good Samaritan who simply passed by. But how to do this? I am reminded of the story of a young man of twenty-two who was suffering from depression. I'm not talking about a religious, but a young man who lived with his mother, who was a widow and who did the laundry for wealthy families. This young man had stopped going to work, and he lived a life clouded by alcohol. His mother couldn't do anything to help him. Every morning before going out, she looked at him with such tenderness. Today, this young man is an important person. He has overcome that problem because that look of tenderness from his mother made an impact on him. We must recover tenderness, even a maternal tenderness. Think of the tenderness that Saint Francis experienced, for example. Tenderness helps overcome conflicts. And if this is not enough, it may be necessary to change communities.

"It is true," Francis continued,

that sometimes we are very cruel. We experience the common temptation to criticize one another for personal satisfaction or for personal advantage. Sometimes the problems of fraternity are due to fragile personalities, and in these kinds of cases, the help of a professional, a psychologist, should be sought. Don't be afraid of this; one should not be overly concerned about falling into an overemphasis on psychology. But we can never, never act simply as managers in the face of a brother's conflict; we have to involve the heart.

Fraternity is very delicate. In the Argentine breviary, the hymn assigned to first Vespers for the Solemnity of Saint Joseph asks Joseph to guard the church with *ternura de eucaristía*— with "Eucharistic tenderness."[14] This is how brothers must be treated: with eucharistic tenderness. Conflict must be cherished. I recall that Pope Paul VI received a letter from a child with several drawings. The pope commented that his desk was filled with letters about various problems and that the arrival of a letter like this did him so much good. Tenderness is good for us. Eucharistic tenderness does not hide from conflict; it helps us to face it like people.

THE RELATIONSHIP BETWEEN RELIGIOUS AND LOCAL CHURCHES

At this point, the superiors general asked the pope some questions about the role of religious communities in local churches and about their relationship with bishops. "How can the charisms of the various orders be respected and contribute to the good of the local church? How can communion be promoted between the distinct charisms and forms of Christian life for the greater growth of all and for more effective mission work?"

Pope Francis replied that there had been a request to review the 1978 document "Directives for the Mutual Relations between Bishops and Religious in the Church"

(*Mutuae Relationes*), issued by the Congregation for Religious and Secular Institutes and the Congregation for Bishops. The pope said he believes the time for a revision is ripe because "that document is set in the context of a certain time and is no longer relevant. The charisms of the various orders must be respected and promoted because they are needed in the dioceses. I know from experience the problems that can arise between the bishop and religious communities." For example, he said,

> If one day a religious order decides to leave a particular ministry due to a lack of vocations, the bishop often suddenly finds himself with a hot potato in his hands. I have had difficult experiences like this. I was told that the ministry was about to be abandoned, and I didn't know what to do. Once I was not even informed until it had already happened. But on the other hand, I could offer other very positive examples.
>
> In short, I know the problems, but I also know that the bishops don't always understand the charisms and the ministries of religious. We bishops must understand that consecrated persons are not tools to be used; they are gifts that enrich our dioceses. The integration of religious communities in a diocese is important. Dialogue between bishop and religious must be maintained in order to avoid a situation where the bishop, not understanding the charisms, consider religious simply to be useful tools.

The pope therefore entrusted the Congregation for Institutes of Consecrated Life and Societies of Apostolic Life with the task of thinking further about a revision of the document *Mutuae Relationes*.

THE FRONTIERS OF MISSION: MARGINALIZATION, CULTURE, AND EDUCATION

The final questions posed to the pope were about the frontiers of mission for consecrated men and women. The pope has often spoken of the church's call to "go forth" into the world, to go to "the frontiers." The superiors general asked him about these frontiers. "How do you understand the presence of consecrated life within the realities of exclusion that exist in our world? Many orders carry out an educational task. How do you see this kind of service? What would you say to religious who are engaged in this field?"

The pope first affirmed that geographical frontiers certainly remain, and that we must be available for mobility. But there are also symbolic frontiers that are not predetermined and not the same for everyone; these, he said,

> must be identified on the basis of the charism of each order. Everything must be discerned in relation to the charism in question. Certainly the realities of exclusion remain the most significant

priorities, but they require discernment. The first criterion is to send the best, most gifted people into these situations of exclusion and marginalization. These are situations of greater risk that require courage and a lot of prayer. And it is necessary that the superior supports the people involved in this work.

There is always the risk, the pope noted, of letting oneself be taken up by enthusiasm, of sending religious who are well-intentioned but who are not suitable for a particular situation in a marginalized frontier. Decisions about ministry to marginalized peoples should not be made without adequate discernment and accompaniment.

Along with the challenge of marginalization, the pope mentioned two other challenges that are always important: culture and education. In these areas, consecrated life can offer an enormous service. Francis recalled,

When the priests of *La Civiltà Cattolica* came to visit me, I spoke to them[15] about the frontiers of thought, ways of thinking that are unique and weak. I recommended these frontiers to them, just as the rector major of the Salesians knows that everything for them started from a dream of education on the frontiers, the dream of Don Bosco that pushed his Salesians to the geographical peripheries of Patagonia. We could give other examples.

The pope noted that for him, the pillars of education are "transmitting knowledge, transmitting ways of doing things, transmitting values. Through these, faith is transmitted. The educator must be up to the task of educating. He must understand how to proclaim Jesus Christ to a changing generation." Then he insisted, "The educational task today is a key, key, key mission!" He recalled some of his experiences in Buenos Aires with welcoming, in educational contexts, young people who live in complex situations, especially in the family.

> I remember the case of a very sad girl who finally confided to her teacher the reason she was troubled: "My mother's fiancé doesn't love me." The percentage of schoolchildren whose parents are separated is very high. The situations we face today therefore pose new challenges that are sometimes even difficult for us to understand. How do we proclaim Christ to these boys and girls? How do we announce Christ to this changing generation? We must be careful not to give them a vaccine against faith.[16]

After three hours, at around 12:30 p.m., the pope apologized for having to bring the conversation to a close. "We leave more questions for next time," he said with a smile. He confided to those present that the dentist was waiting for him.

Before greeting the superiors general present, he announced that 2015 would be observed in the church as a special year dedicated to consecrated life. This was greeted with long applause. Now the pope looked with a smile at the prefect and the secretary of the Congregation for Institutes of Consecrated Life and Societies of Apostolic Life, and said, "It's their fault. It was their idea. When these two get together, they're dangerous," causing the whole assembly to erupt in laughter.

Before leaving the hall, the pope said,

Thank you, thank you for this leap of faith that you have made at this meeting. Thank you for what you do, for your spirit of faith and the pursuit of service. Thank you for your witness, for the martyrs you continually give to the church, and also for the humiliations you have to endure—it is the path of the cross. Thank you so much.

2

POPE FRANCIS'S EIGHT CHALLENGES FOR CONSECRATED LIFE

Antonio Spadaro, SJ

Pope Francis, as a Jesuit religious, was able to open his 2014 letter to all consecrated persons with these words: "I am…writing to you as a brother who, like yourselves, is consecrated to God."[1] Jorge Bergoglio began his novitiate in the Society of Jesus on March 11, 1958, and he went on to become, first, novice master and, later, provincial.

The audience with the USG described above was the first opportunity for Bergoglio, after his election as pope, to clearly affirm and share his identity as a consecrated person. But that conversation bears important connections to reflections he had offered earlier in his life and also to some that followed.

Having considered the November 2013 dialogue between the pope and the superiors general, our task now is to consider some of the challenges that Francis poses to consecrated religious in the light of these and other observations.

BISHOP BERGOGLIO AT THE 1994 SYNOD

We'll start with comments offered by Jorge Bergoglio in 1994, when he was auxiliary bishop of Buenos Aires. The setting was the ninth ordinary general assembly of the Synod of Bishops, dedicated to the theme "The Consecrated Life and Its Role in the Church and in the World." On that occasion he made an interesting contribution to the synod's reflection on consecrated life. In his intervention to the synod fathers, he began by saying that consecrated life must be understood in its "multiform aspect."[2] Adapting one of the images that has long been important to him, he noted that consecrated life is not to be understood as a sphere, but as a polyhedron. By employing this image, Bergoglio's intention is to bypass ideals or abstract utopias that are given an evangelical flavor, in order to draw attention instead to the tensions that are "inherent in the diverse richness that is found in ecclesial life." To the bishops at the synod, he noted three such tensions: "1. Tension between the religious order and the holy and faithful people of God. 2. Tension between an order's particular charism and the needs of the world. 3. Tension underlying the experience of insertion."[3]

Having noted these, the auxiliary bishop of Buenos Aires went on to elaborate upon them. Here we quote his comments at length (with the first two observations relating to the first of his three points):

1. With regard to the first tension, I wish to underline only one aspect: the sense of the faith of God's faithful people. Our faithful people, as a body, bear this intuitive sense. This is the *sensus Ecclesiae* and the *sensus Christi*. And the church has insisted upon its infallibility. The faithful people of God "cannot err in matters of belief" (*Lumen Gentium* 12). The hierarchy "cannot err in matters of teaching." A religious family, through the tensions inherent in multiformity, participates in this sense of the holy people of God.

2. With respect to the tension between the particular church and the universal church, Pope John Paul II told the superiors general on November 24, 1978, "Wherever you are in the world, you are, with your vocation, 'for *the universal Church*,' through your mission '*in a given local Church*.'"[4]

3. Regarding the third tension, I say that we must not allow the needs of the world to push

us to standardize the diversity of charisms in ways that do them harm, nor may we hide the charisms behind a distinctive style that prevents us from seeing or dealing with the world's needs. A constant deuteronomic attitude is required of us, demanding that we commit ourselves here and now. In this regard, we must keep in mind that a poor resolution of this tension leads to functionalism and to an attitude of spiritual worldliness that destroys consecrated life.

4. The fourth tension is that consecrated life cannot ignore the concept of insertion. The tension here is between the life we are living now and its eschatological dimension. To be inserted means to follow the example of being limited (in time and space) from the incarnation of the Word all the way to the threshold of the most intense drama, so intense as to constitute it—qualitatively—absolutely, overcoming time and space.[5]

A CHARISM IS FOR THE BUILDING UP OF THE CHURCH

What is the meaning of this brief but incisive intervention? Bergoglio means first of all that a religious family's place is in the midst of the people and that it fully participates in the *sensus fidelium*. It is a part the people of God, within a local church but with its universal vocation. The test of each of the various charisms is therefore precisely the building up of the church, the common good (cf. 1 Cor 12:7).

From within the church, religious women and men listen to the needs of the world. For this reason, they must avoid two dangers. On the one hand, they mustn't hide behind the particularism of their own charism and mission in a way that prevents them even from seeing real needs. On the other hand, they mustn't look at the needs outside the context of their own charism, which only leads to standardizing and flattening diversity. This is the tension between charism and mission.

However, the insertion of religious into the reality of life is always accompanied by an eschatological gaze: religious life brings the fragment into the whole, sees what is limited within its eternal context. And this generates a strong tension, which the religious feels in her very skin. Pope Francis has recalled this tension repeatedly. For him, eschatological tension is the truest and most profound decentralization, because Christ, the Beginning and the End, is the only center. He said this, for example, to the Jesuits in 2013[6] and again in a 2015 address to the members of Communion and Liberation. To the latter, he said,

Remember that the center is not the charism, the center is one alone, it is Jesus, Jesus Christ!

When I place at the center my spiritual method, my spiritual journey, my way of fulfilling it, I go off the itinerary. All spirituality, all charisms in the Church must be "decentralized": at the center there is only the Lord![7]

Rereading the answers offered by the pope to the questions of the superiors general during the 2013 meeting together with his 1994 synod intervention and some earlier texts on religious life that Bergoglio wrote as provincial of the Argentine Jesuits, one can recognize a set of challenges emerging. We will consider each of these now. We will identify eight, though certainly the list could be much longer. But our intention here is to grasp some fundamental elements.

THE CHALLENGES

1. Recognizing Oneself as a Sinner

During the 2013 USG meeting, the pope told the superiors, "You must truly be witnesses of a different way of acting and living."[8] This is an appeal that is not the least bit "moralistic," but it does express a concept of consecrated life as a life that does not follow worldly principles and values, and that therefore makes the consecrated person stand out because of his or her "differentness." But this doesn't mean that the religious is always successful in living a good and holy life according to the Gospel. And here we find the first challenge—and a central one—for consecrated life.

As we have seen, Francis responded to a question from the superiors by saying,

> In life it is difficult for everything to be clear, precise, clearly drawn. Life is complex; it is made up of grace and sin. *One who does not sin is not a person.* We all make mistakes, and we must recognize our weakness. A religious who recognizes himself as weak and sinful does not contradict the witness he is called to give, but rather strengthens it, and this is good for everyone.[9]

Recognizing oneself as a sinner is the first challenge of consecrated life. It means being realistic about one's identity before God, who shuns all idealism and all moralism. To say that "one who does not sin is not a person" means that sin calls us back to a fundamental identity that the religious must always bear in mind: the need for a radical openness to grace. And the complexity of life must be recognized. His own fragility, viewed with humble eyes, leads not to contradicting the "ideal" of the life he has embraced, but to make that life more true and more human.

To his Jesuit confreres in 2014, the pope spoke similarly:

> We are men in tension, we are also contradictory and inconsistent men, sinners, all of us. But we are men who want to journey under Jesus' gaze. We are small, we are sinners, but we want to

fight under the banner of the Cross in the Society designated by the name of Jesus. We who are selfish want nonetheless to live life aspiring to great deeds.[10]

The identity of sinner is also the most basic description that the pontiff offers of *himself*. "Who is Jorge Mario Bergoglio?" was the first question that I posed to him in the groundbreaking 2013 interview soon after his election. After a pause for reflection, the pontiff slowly replied, "I do not know what might be the most fitting description….I am a sinner. This is the most accurate definition. It is not a figure of speech, a literary genre. I am a sinner." After a pause for thought, he continued, "Yes, perhaps I can say that I am a bit astute, that I can adapt to circumstances, but it is also true that I am a bit naïve. Yes, but the best summary, the one that comes more from the inside and I feel most true is this: I am a sinner whom the Lord has looked upon."[11]

The pope's own self-understanding is that of being a sinful person. But if we read carefully, we see that it is also very much rooted in his experience *specifically as a religious*. In 1974, Fr. Jorge Mario Bergoglio had participated in the twenty-third general congregation of the Society of Jesus. The first decree issued by this world assembly of representatives of the order begins with the question, "What does it mean to be a Jesuit?" And it offers this answer: "It means recognizing oneself as a sinner, but called by God to be a companion of Jesus Christ, as was Ignatius." In other words, in his reply to the 2013 interview question, Pope Francis was not merely speaking about himself in general, but precisely in light of the charism that profoundly touches his identity.

This recognition of one's sin comes together, in Francis's vision, with the perception of an existential restlessness. We see him articulate this, for example, in comments that he offered to members of the Order of Saint Augustine. Preaching at a Mass at the order's general chapter in 2013, the pope said of the saint from whom the order takes its name, "Of course he made mistakes, he took wrong turns, he sinned, he was a sinner. Yet he retained the restlessness of spiritual seeking. In this way he discovered that God was waiting for him, indeed, that he had never ceased to be the first to seek him."[12] Francis's appeal to consecrated persons, then, is to "[confess] humbly, with immense confidence in the God who is Love (cf. 1 Jn 4:8), our own weakness and, in it, to experience the Lord's merciful love."[13]

The first challenge, then, for those who have embraced the consecrated life is this: How does the charism of the order to which one belongs help to understand oneself as a sinner? What specific challenge does it pose starting from the fact that we are aware of being sinful? How is the order's specific spirituality nourished by a healthy spiritual restlessness? In this sense, the richness of all the spiritual forms within Christianity has much to teach us, well before any lofty but abstract ideal of holiness.

2. Seeking and Finding God in All Things

The spirituality of the order to which Pope Francis belongs—Ignatian spirituality—is his charismatic identity and the interpretive key by which he came to understand and integrate his experiences as a priest, then bishop, then pope. At the end of his service as provincial, Jorge Mario Bergoglio collected for publication some of his writings from those years.[14] These are fundamental for understanding his vision of religious life and the roots of his thought in general.

It is interesting to note that Bergoglio chose to dedicate this collection of writings not to a fellow Jesuit, but to a Salesian. Fr. Enrique Pozzoli was a priest who had a fundamental influence in Bergoglio's life. He was a family friend, the confessor and spiritual guide of Jorge's father Mario, and it was Pozzoli who baptized Jorge on Christmas Day 1936 in the basilica of San Carlos Borromeo y María Auxiliadora, in Almagro, Argentina, with his maternal grandmother Rosa and grandfather Francisco at his side.

In the book, then-Fr. Bergoglio described Don Pozzoli in a fascinating way: as a "watchmaker" and as a "photographer." Bergoglio wrote, "He had a fine ear for recognizing the movement of conscience and a portentous eye for impressing God's love in hearts. He knew how to put the intricate landscape of a soul in tune with God's rhythm. He knew how to help others recognize God's plan in their lives."[15]

This is an excellent description of discernment. In the images of watchmaker and photographer, we can recognize already both Bergoglio the Jesuit provincial and Bergoglio the bishop who championed the cause of the *curas villeros*, the "slum priests" of Buenos Aires. We also recognize the rector of the Jesuit formation house who—as we know from the testimonies of his confreres—pushed young religious to work with the poor, but who also sent them on Sundays to the Teatro Colón, a prestigious Buenos Aires opera house, because he believed that both activities would help to form their hearts to understand the rhythms of human conscience.

There, in the grime of the *villas miserias* and in the luxurious opera house, they had to learn to recognize the presence of God. The consecrated person must be ready to seek and find God in all things and situations, with an attentive heart and eye. It is a pastoral challenge, but also a profoundly spiritual one. What is at stake is the soul's ability to recognize God, not where our senses expect to find him, but where God decides to be and to act.

Returning our attention to Bergoglio's comments on Don Pozzoli, we also note that he does not intend with the metaphor of "photographer" to depict Pozzoli as one who, with his lens, captures images of reality as it is, but rather as one who is able to impress on the film of the human heart the light and colors of God's love. Bergoglio's image is intended to refer to the "film," and the eye of the consecrated person is the photographic "lens" that conveys the light on it.

That is the second challenge: the ability to discern the presence of God in history and not in ideas. This relates to the tension that Bergoglio identified in the 1994 synod, between the response to the needs of everyday life and the breadth of the charism in the light of which it is necessary to discern mission.

3. Having an Open Mind

"The Jesuit must be a person whose thought is incomplete, in the sense of open-ended thinking," Pope Francis said in his interview with *La Civiltà Cattolica*. He continued, saying that "the Jesuit always thinks, again and again, looking at the horizon toward which he must go, with Christ at the center. This is his real strength. And that pushes the Society to be searching, creative, and generous."[16]

Having Christ at the center opens up our thought, because it is directed toward a horizon to which it remains open. The question that the consecrated person therefore asks himself in the world is, "How would Christ have acted in this case?" There is no slavish application of a "rule" of life, but simply a disciple who constantly sets his eyes on the Teacher. In this way, he is always open to life's surprises and new challenges.

Calling to mind Saint Peter Faber during the celebration of Mass in the church of the Gesù shortly after canonizing him, the pope offered him as a model of this tension that led Faber to feel "the desire to 'allow Christ to occupy the center of his heart.' It is only possible to go to the limits of the world if we are centered in God!"[17]

Open-ended thinking pushes consecrated persons to live in the peripheries. Francis wrote in his letter to consecrated persons,

> I also expect from you what I have asked all the members of the Church: to come out of yourselves and go forth to the existential peripheries. "Go into all the world"; these were the last words which Jesus spoke to his followers and which he continues to address to us (cf. Mark 16:15). A whole world awaits us.

And then rather than being vague, the pope offered a catalog of what he means by "the peripheries" of the world: "men and women who have lost all hope, families in difficulty, abandoned children, young people without a future, the elderly, sick and abandoned, those who are rich in the world's goods but impoverished within, men and women looking for a purpose in life, thirsting for the divine." He went on,

> I ask you to work concretely in welcoming refugees, drawing near to the poor, and finding creative ways to catechize, to proclaim the Gospel and to teach others how to pray. Consequently, I would hope that structures can be streamlined, large religious houses repurposed for works which better respond to the present demands

of evangelization and charity, and apostolates adjusted to new needs.[18]

Going to the peripheries also means listening to the needs they express. "Saint Ignatius," Bergoglio wrote many years ago, "was not afraid to contemplate reality; indeed he knew that 'it is to this world that we are sent: its needs and aspirations are an appeal launched in the direction of the Gospel that we have the mission to proclaim.'"[19]

When we listen to Francis speaking to us about the church going forth into the world and missionary conversion, we should remember these words of decades ago. The needs of the world represent the world's appeal to the Gospel. Those who engage in pastoral care are often used to thinking the other way around, that is, to consider the appeal that the Gospel makes to the world, to its people. The dynamic of those who live a religious charism is first of all that of having the sensitivity to hear "the cry of the people" toward God (cf. Exod 3:9) and to understand how the word of God is to be proclaimed precisely in the context of that cry.

After all, as the pope has told us, "we should never respond to questions that nobody asks."[20] For this reason, our thought must always be "open-ended" and never willing to create short circuits of purely and abstractly doctrinal reasoning. The *salus animarum* always remains the *suprema lex* of the church, as we read in the final canon, number 1752, of the Code of Canon Law.

What emerges here is the idea of a consecrated life that is immersed in the noises of this world but capable of finding in the midst of them the silence of peace and consolation, which is God himself. It is not in a formal *fuga mundi* that the consecrated person finds the Lord. Indeed, as we have seen in Francis's comments to the USG, "The ghost that we must fight is the image of religious life as a refuge and consolation from a difficult and complex 'outside' world."[21] For this reason, the church's identity is inseparable from its mission. The church, as a living reality, becomes aware of itself—as an individual person does—through its own experience, through living its life and listening to the needs of the people. For this reason, it is not exempt from the efforts necessary for a well-developed self-understanding.

For Francis, the world is always in motion, and so the church also must be; the ordinary perspective, with its yardsticks for classifying what is important and what is not, does not work. The life of the spirit has other criteria. The principle that summarizes this vision is articulated in the famous sepulchral epitaph of Saint Ignatius, *Non coerceri maximo, contineri tamen a minima, divinum est*, which could be translated, "Not to be confined to what is greater, but to be concerned with what is smaller: this is divine." This motto is very dear to Bergoglio; he quotes it often. He took it up, for example, in his homily for the consistory of February 14, 2015. On this occasion he spoke of the importance of patience:

> The greater our responsibility in serving the Church, the more our hearts must expand

according to the measure of the heart of Christ. "Patience"—"forbearance"—is in some sense synonymous with catholicity. It means being able to love without limits, but also to be faithful in particular situations and with practical gestures. It means loving what is great without neglecting what is small; loving the little things within the horizon of the great things, since *"non coerceri a maximo, contineri tamen a minimo divinum est."*[22]

These words reveal the Bergoglian vision of those who consecrate themselves to God and to God's service, who must be people with an open mind and a patient heart. Being able to recognize the divine in the smallest things and rather than only in great things is a fundamental criterion.

Without this immersion in the particular reality of the universal charism, a priest becomes a sort of consecrated "acrobat," who "in his coming and going can no longer remain founded in God and in the concrete history with which he is associated." Or he will develop "grandiose plans with no attention to the concrete steps necessary that will have to implement them well." Or it could cause him to become stranded "in the small events and details of every passing moment without seeing them in the context of the plan of God that transcends them."[23] Clearly, this is the tension that Bergoglio was referring to in his comments at the 1994 synod meeting, between the local, particular dimension of the life and mission of the religious and the universal dimension of her charism.[24]

God is "always greater"—for Ignatius as for Bergoglio. God's plan is greater than our own personal projects.[25] The process is therefore truly open-ended; only God knows its conclusion and fruit. It is much broader and much more than any human project, and it exceeds all our expectations. Bergoglio offers an effective image drawn from the Gospels. "We are encouraged," he wrote during his provincial years, "to build the city, but perhaps we will have to tear down the model we had drawn in our heads. We must take courage and let the chisel of God represent our face, even if the blows cancel some tics that we thought were gestures."[26] The *pars destruens*, the destructive parts, that consist of breaking down the "model," are necessary in order for us to trust the chisel in God's hand. It's an idea that helps us understand Francis's way of being pope. And this is also *the third great challenge* that the pope poses to consecrated persons: an open mind capable of being concrete, that is, being incarnate.

4. Being Prophets

The church must be attractive. Wake up the world! Be witnesses of a different way of doing, of acting, of living! It is possible to live differently in this world. We are talking about an eschatological gaze, about the values of the kingdom embodied here, on this earth. It is about leaving everything to follow the Lord. No, I don't mean it's about religious living "radically." The radicalism of the Gospel is not only for religious; it is required of all. But religious follow the Lord in a special way, in a prophetic way. I expect this witness from you. Religious must be men and women capable of waking up the world.[27]

These, as we have already seen, are the words of Pope Francis to the superiors general. They make a clear distinction between "radicalism" and prophecy. The religious *is* radical, as every true Christian must be, but more distinctively, she leads a life that embodies a prophecy to which some are called by vocation. It is

the prophecy of the kingdom, which is not negotiable. The emphasis must fall on being prophets, and not on playing at being one. Of course, the devil presents his temptations to us, and this is one of them: playing at being prophets without being one, assuming their attitudes. But you can't pretend in these things. I myself have seen very sad things in this regard. No—consecrated religious are men and women who illuminate the future.[28]

Within this appeal to prophecy lies the tension that Bergoglio identified at the 1994 synod, between our present lives and the eschatological dimension that the religious embodies, sometimes dramatically. In his interview with *La Civiltà Cattolica*, Francis expressed the call of religious women and men to a prophetic life. This is their distinctive characteristic:

> In the church, the religious are called to be prophets in particular by demonstrating how Jesus lived on this earth, and to proclaim how the kingdom of God will be in its perfection. A religious must never give up prophecy....Let us think about what so many great saints, monks and religious men and women have done, from St. Anthony the Abbot onward. Being prophets may sometimes imply making waves. I do not know how to put it....Prophecy makes noise, uproar, some say "a mess." But in reality, the charism of religious people is like yeast: prophecy announces the spirit of the Gospel.[29]

Pope Francis's proposal is "prophetic" in the sense that Yves Congar defined the term, that is, carried out by those who "reveal the meaning of time and of the initiatives and movements that arise in history principally from the point of view of God and God's plan."[30] This is why Pope Francis has reminded consecrated men and woman of the need to "read the signs of the times with the eyes of faith and to respond creatively to the needs of the Church."[31]

Precisely in the service of prophecy, it is necessary "to strengthen what is institutional in consecrated life and not to confuse the religious order with the particular apostolic work."[32] In fact the first remains, the second passes. The order—that is, its charism—is the real mine that is always open and teeming, while its concrete and historical implementations vary with time; one must not try to crystallize or stiffen what is dynamic and fluid by nature. What is prophetic today may not be in a different historical moment. The charism is creative; it is always looking for new ways.[33] It cannot be "bottled" or "petrified": "The charism is not preserved in a bottle of distilled water! Faithfulness to the charism does not mean 'to petrify it'—the devil is the one who 'petrifies,' do not forget! Faithfulness to the charism does not mean to write it on a parchment and frame it."[34]

Precisely for this reason, it is important not just to speak of charism in abstract terms, but "to tell our story."[35] It is through such self-narration that identity is kept alive. Indeed, "when you express too much, you run the risk of being misunderstood....Only in narrative form do you discern, not in a philosophical or theological explanation, which allows you rather to discuss."[36]

Here, then, is the fourth challenge: How to be a prophet while living one's own particular religious charism within history? The pope offers some elements of the answer: an eschatological lifestyle marked by generosity, detachment, sacrifice, and self-forgetfulness; creativity; authenticity that avoids playing at being prophets; being yeast in the dough; giving "warning signs" to people who have forgotten what is at stake.

5. Being Generative

One grave risk to religious life is sterility. More generally, if the church is a mother, it cannot fail to generate the life of its children. But if the church closes in on itself, it becomes sterile, unsuitable for life. And so the church's shepherds are and must be fathers and guides. And yet, Bergoglio observed wryly, "there are men who started out by promising to shepherd a flock and who end up stroking angora cats."[37] Generativity is the characteristic of mother church. So the question of the survival of a religious order lies in its choice "either for fecundity or for sterility." And being fruitful is about "the mystery of fatherhood in faith," which "substantially represents the mystery of the divine gift that gives fruitfulness to whomever God wills."[38] There is no fruitfulness in faith if one does not allow God to act in the way God chooses.

At the heart of this paternal vision is God himself:

He is not an absent figure. He is the father who accompanies our growth, the daily bread that nourishes us, the merciful one who accompanies us in the moments when the Enemy uses us his children. He is the father who, when it's fitting, gives his child what he asks for, but even when he doesn't always gives caresses.[39]

This paternity flows from one of the characteristics of every founder of a religious order: fruitfulness. Indeed, "the grace received, which prompts a particular way of serving God, is destined simultaneously for the bene-fit of both the founder and others. And it is transmit-ted to her or his daughters or sons."[40]

The novitiate, therefore,

> is not an academy where one goes "to learn about the order." It is not a laboratory experiment. It is "entering a family." Its purpose is to give the young religious who is initiated a set of truths that are felt before they are understood and that constitute a philosophy of a life. We call this core of truth doctrine, and its source is the deposit of faith, the living tradition of the church, the mag-isterium, and our specific tradition as an order. And the mission of the formator resides, first of all, in inculcating a doctrinal nucleus in the heart of the one being formed and in teaching her to understand it.[41]

Spiritual doctrine is not an abstract system of ideas, an ideological scaffolding, or a "sack" of truths to carry on one's shoulders; it is a set of truths first heard and then understood that shape a life.

This, then, is the fifth great challenge: to be people who live "looking fruitfully towards the future and offering clear answers to the present. This is a very different attitude compared to those who take refuge in 'it has always been done this way.'"[42]

A frequent temptation in the church is instead what Bergoglio describes as the "spirituality of the ostrich." It consists in wanting to hide one's head by taking ref-

uge either in a "restoration workshop," as traditional-
ists would like, or in a "utopian laboratory," as would
like those who try to always stay on the crest of the
wave, *à la page*.[43]

Retrograde traditionalism and progressive utopi-
anism are the worst impediments to a fruitful, generative attitude. In short, if consecrated life becomes
an ideology—either conservative or progressive—it
becomes sterile. And thus, writing to consecrated
persons, Francis reiterated, "I trust that, rather than
living in some utopia, you will find ways to create
'alternate spaces,' where the Gospel approach of self-
giving, fraternity, embracing differences, and love of
one another can thrive."[44]

This is why, when speaking with the superiors general, the pope insisted that formation must be oriented
not only to personal growth, but also to its ultimate
goal: the people of God. Here is a decisive point for
the evaluation of a formational journey. Francis said,

> We must always think of the faithful, the faithful
> people of God. We have to form people who are
> witnesses of the resurrection of Jesus. The for-
> mator must remember that the person in forma-
> tion will be called to care for the people of God.
> We must always think of the people of God, as
> one of them. Let us recall those religious who
> have hearts as acidic as vinegar: they are not
> made for the people. In short, we must not form
> administrators or managers, but fathers, broth-
> ers, companions on the journey.[45]

The pope's approach is not functionalistic. He insists that religious life is not a "bubble" within the people of God, within the church. When Bergoglio told the bishops gathered at the 1994 synod that a religious family participates in the "sense" of the holy people of God, he meant, among other things, that the bishop's ministry must be founded upon his own participation in this sense. He must therefore keep at the forefront of his mind not just the individual in formation or ministry and that person's formative needs, as if they were personal needs abstract from an ecclesial context. Only by attentiveness to those to whom consecrated persons will be sent is it possible to "generate" and form the religious in the charism.

And it is precisely in this way that communities of consecrated persons become generative "families." Bergoglio said, again in his 1994 speech, that "one cannot reflect on consecrated life except from within the church, underlining the inter-ecclesial relationship that this implies." Indeed, "consecrated life is a gift to the church, it is born in the church, it grows in the church, and it is entirely oriented to the church."[46]

In his 2014 letter to consecrated persons, the pope echoed the intervention he'd offered at the synod twenty years earlier, even quoting it, telling his readers that they are at the very heart of the church as a decisive element of its mission. And with an eye to the founders of their orders, the pope asked them, "Do we have the same passion for our people, are we close to them to the point of sharing in their joys and sorrows, thus truly understanding their needs and helping to respond to them?"[47]

6. Being Brothers

"At times we can live in a building without knowing our next door neighbor; or we can be in a community without really knowing our own confreres: I think sorrowfully of the consecrated people who are infertile 'old bachelors,'" the pope said at the Augustinian general chapter in 2013.[48] One aspect of generativity is the ability to develop fraternal relationships, to give life in a particular sense to a family experience. And this is not an easy undertaking, because there is always the possibility of conflict. But "religious fraternity, in all its possible variations, is an experience of love that goes beyond conflicts."[49]

We know well that one of the pillars of the pontiff's thought is that unity is superior to conflict. But unity is not achieved by covering or preventing conflict. It is reached by embracing multiplicity, just as musical harmony is reached through the reconciliation of dissonances. The religious fraternity experienced by consecrated persons is not the fruit of an ideal tension that blinds us to unreconciled differences and interpersonal conflicts. Indeed, as we have seen,

> community conflicts are inevitable; in a certain sense, they must exist if the community truly lives sincere and loyal relationships. That's life. Imagining a community without brothers who

sometimes have difficulties makes no sense, and it is not good. If there is no conflict in a community, it means something is missing. Reality tells us that there's conflict in all families and in all human groups. And conflict must be faced; it can't be ignored. If it is covered up, it creates pressure and then explodes. A life without conflict is not real life.[50]

Conflict is part of any real life. Just as there is no person who doesn't sin, so there is no community that does not argue. It is important to understand that Francis thinks of religious communities in terms of family—a "charismatic family"—and of a "common sense of belonging."[51] And in families, siblings cannot help but quarrel, in a certain sense. Friction is proof of real contact.

However, the conflict must be accompanied: "We must never behave like the priest or the Levite in the parable of the Good Samaritan who simply pass by....We can never, never act simply as managers in the face of a brother's conflict; we have to involve the heart."[52] Bergoglio makes a clear distinction between "companion" and "manager." There is a temptation in communities to manage people in order to exercise control over the situation, but this fails to fully respect the humanity of community life.

Fraternity is something "very delicate," the pope told the USG is 2013; and *this is a sixth great challenge that the pope offers to religious.* "In the Argentine breviary, the hymn assigned to first vespers for the Solemnity of Saint Joseph asks Joseph to guard the church with *ternura de eucaristía*—with 'Eucharistic tenderness.'" This, the pope said, is how religious must treat one another. "Conflict must be cherished.... Eucharistic tenderness does not cover the conflict; it helps us to face it as men."[53]

7. Going on Mission

The pope certainly recognizes that there are geographical borders, and the nonmonastic religious must be available for mobility. But there are also symbolic frontiers, which are not predetermined, not the same for everyone, and therefore "must be identified on the basis of the charism of each order. Everything must be discerned in relation to the charism in question."[54] Mission is not a phase that comes subsequent to the spiritual charism, nor a secondary expression of it. Just as the church has learned to understand itself in its history and mission, so the charisms of the orders are understood through their historical expression of the service of the people of God on pilgrimage. In this mission, the prophetic and eschatological nature of the vocation to consecrated life pushes us toward frontiers.

Speaking in 2013 to the Jesuits who produce the journal *La Civiltà Cattolica*, Francis addressed this clearly:

> Your proper place is at the frontier. This is the place of Jesuits. Today too what Paul VI said about the Society of Jesus, taken up by Benedict

XVI, applies in a particular way to you: "Wherever in the Church, even in the most difficult and extreme fields, at the crossroads of ideologies, in the social trenches, there has been and there is confrontation between the burning exigencies of man and the perennial message of the Gospel, here also there have been, and there are, Jesuits."

Please be pioneers empowered by God (cf. 2 Cor 3:6). But do not give in to the temptation of domesticating these frontiers: it is essential to go out to the frontiers but not to bring frontiers home to touch them up with a little varnish and tame them.[55]

For the missionary, the pope offers this vision: to be at the crossroads and confront the burning needs of humanity. When Francis speaks of the church with open doors, he certainly means a church that opens its doors to let people in, but even before that he means a church that opens the doors to let the Lord out and not try to hold him prisoner inside.[56] This is the "church that goes forth" that he calls us to be.

Speaking to Catholics of Rome in 2013, the pope recalled the passage of the Gospel about the shepherd who left the ninety-nine sheep to go out in search of the one that was lost. "But brothers and sisters," Francis said, "we have one sheep. We have lost the other ninety-nine!…In this culture—let us tell the truth—we only have one, we are a minority!" And he asked them, "Do we feel the fervor, the apostolic zeal to go out and find the other ninety-nine?"[57]

For religious, the pope told the USG,

> certainly the realities of exclusion remain the
> most significant priorities, but they require dis-
> cernment. The first criterion is to send the best,
> most gifted people into these situations of exclu-
> sion and marginalization. These are situations
> of greater risk that require courage and a lot
> of prayer. And it is necessary that the superior
> accompanies the people involved in this work.[58]

There is always a risk, the pope recalled, of being
taken up by enthusiasm, of sending religious who are
well-intentioned but unsuitable for ministry to marginalized frontiers. Decisions should not be made
regarding ministry to people who are marginalized
without adequate discernment and accompaniment.

In addition to this challenge of marginalization, as
we have seen, the pope is keen to point out two other
challenges that are always important: one of culture, the
other of education. In this area, consecrated life can
offer an enormous service. "The educator must be up to
the task of educating. He must understand how to proclaim Jesus Christ to a changing generation," he said.
"The educational task today is a key, key, key mission!"[59]
With the USB members, the pope recalled some of his
experiences in Buenos Aires that taught him the
importance of welcoming in educational contexts
young people who live in complex situations, especially
in the family:

I remember the case of a very sad girl who finally confided to her teacher the reason she was troubled: "My mother's fiancé doesn't love me." The percentage of schoolchildren whose parents are separated is very high. The situations we face today therefore pose new challenges that are sometimes even difficult for us to understand. How do we proclaim Christ to these boys and girls? How do we announce Christ to this changing generation? We must be careful not to give them a vaccine against faith.[60]

What is especially striking about Francis's approach as he expressed it in November 2013 is the fact that he identifies the challenges by name. In this case, the pope refers to a question: How to proclaim the Gospel to children of incomplete, imperfect, wounded, or even same-sex families? Naming this pastoral challenge in such explicit terms was unthinkable just a few years ago. If reality isn't named, especially in the most complex challenges, mission work will not be effective, because people and their problems will go unrecognized. *This is the seventh great challenge* that we call attention to here.

8. The Challenge of Joy and Consolation

Let's give our attention to one final challenge—that of spiritual consolation—by considering three moments in which Francis addressed it.

During the Angelus of December 7, 2014, the pope said,

> It is curious, but many times we are afraid of con-solation, of being comforted. Or rather, we feel more secure in sorrow and desolation. Do you know why? Because in sorrow we feel almost as protagonists. However, in consolation the Holy Spirit is the protagonist! It is He who consoles us, it is He who gives us the courage to go out of ourselves. It is He who opens the door to the source of every true comfort, that is, the Father. And this is conversion. Please, let yourselves be comforted by the Lord! Let yourselves be com-forted by the Lord![61]

The pope, especially when speaking extemporane-ously, doesn't hesitate to speak of the importance of consolation. The mission of the church is one of con-solation. During a 2014 apostolic journey to Albania, after listening in the Cathedral of Tirana to the testi-mony of two people—a priest and a religious—who had suffered for their faith, he said extemporane-ously,

> We, who have been called by the Lord to follow him closely, must find our consolation in him alone. Woe to us if we seek consolation elsewhere! Woe to priests and religious, sisters and novices, consecrated men and women, when they seek consolation far from the Lord! Today I don't want

to be harsh and severe with you, but I want you to realize very clearly that if you look for consolation anywhere else, you will not be happy! Even more, you will be unable to comfort others, for your own heart is closed to the Lord's consolation. You will end up, as the great Elijah said to the people of Israel, "limping with both legs."[62]

Finally, in a spontaneous and unofficial dialogue with Jesuits that took place in Seoul during his 2014 apostolic journey to Korea, Pope Francis said,

There is a word that I think about a lot: consolation....The people of God need consolation, need to be consoled, the *consuelo*. I think the church is a field hospital right now. God's people ask us to be consoled. So many wounds, so many wounds that need consolation....We must listen to the word of Isaiah: "Comfort, comfort my people!" There are no wounds that cannot be consoled by the love of God. We must live in this way: looking for Jesus Christ in order to bring this love to console the wounds, to heal the wounds....There are many wounds in the church. Wounds that we, practicing Catholics and ministers of the church, often cause ourselves. Do not chastise God's people anymore! Comfort the people of God! Many times our clerical attitude causes clericalism, which does so much damage to the church. Being a priest does make a person a senior official, but a shepherd. Please be shepherds and not senior officials. And when you are in the confessional, remember that God never tires of forgiving. Be merciful![63]

These three passages make it clear that consolation is truly a challenge, because allowing oneself to be consoled means letting God act rather than acting ourselves. When Francis speaks of a decentralization from oneself, it also means letting go of one's feelings of sadness and desolation and letting God comfort us. And this is perhaps the greatest missionary and apostolic challenge because "we cannot be messengers of God's comfort if we do not first feel the joy of being comforted and loved by Him."[64] It is precisely spiritual consolation that is *an eighth important challenge, capable of touching the deep chords of the soul.* It is the challenge capable of effectively supporting the prophetic dynamism that is the central characteristic of religious life.

RELIGIOUS LIFE AS A "CARAVAN"

We have identified eight challenges for consecrated life as they emerge from Bergoglio's thought as priest, bishop, and then pope. They are the following: recognizing ourselves as sinners saved by grace; the discernment that seeks and finds God in all things; open-ended thinking; prophecy; generativity; fraternity; mission.

From these quick brushstrokes emerges the portrait of a complex and multifaceted life in its opportunities and challenges. Certainly a life worth living.

If we were to seek an ecclesial image to describe consecrated life, it would need to be capable of adequately representing the richness of this life, in all its lights and shadows. Perhaps we could not do better than that of a *caravan*—a "caravan of solidarity"—which Francis himself used in his 2014 apostolic letter to all consecrated persons, and which he took up again later the same year in his apostolic exhortation *Evangelii Gaudium*. It illustrates not only "a different way of doing,"[65] but also its challenges and positive tensions. Francis wrote, "We sense the challenge of finding and sharing a 'mystique' of living together, of mingling and encounter, of embracing and supporting one another, of stepping into this flood tide which, while chaotic, can become a genuine experience of fraternity, a caravan of solidarity, a sacred pilgrimage."[66]

"THE GOSPEL WITHOUT SEDATIVES"

A Conversation between Pope Francis and the Superiors General

"The pope is late," they told me at the entrance to the Paul VI Audience Hall. It was Friday morning, November 25, 2016. A light rain was falling. Waiting inside this building, known best as the setting for papal audiences and meetings of the Synod of Bishops, were 140 members of the Union of Superiors General (USG), leaders of the world's male religious orders. They were gathered to conclude their eighty-eighth general assembly, which had been held for the past three days at Rome's Pontifical Salesian University (known more commonly as the Salesianum) under the theme "Go and Bear Fruit: The Fruitfulness of Prophecy."

It is uncommon for the pope to arrive late. At 10:15 a.m., the photographers arrived and then the pope walked in briskly. After the applause of greeting, Francis began: "Forgive the delay. That's how life is, full of surprises. To understand God's surprises, one must understand those that life sends us. Thank you very much." He continued by saying that he didn't want his delay to shorten the time he was able to spend with the group. And so the meeting lasted three hours as previously planned.

At the halfway point, there was a break. A room had been prepared as a place for the pope to be able to take some time to himself, but he objected, saying, "Why do you want me to be all alone?" And so he spent the break with the superiors general, greeting them, talking, and enjoying a coffee and snack.

There were no prepared speeches by either the superiors or the pope. Videographers were present to record the initial greetings and then they left, allowing the meeting to have a free and fraternal atmosphere, with both questions and answers that were unfiltered. The pope had rejected the idea of screening questions in advance. After listening to a very brief greeting and introduction from Fr. Mauro Jöhri, the USG president and minister general of the Order of Friars Minor Capuchin, and Fr. David Glenday, the USG general secretary and a Comboni Missionary, the pope was ready to listen to questions offered by members of the group.

And if they included criticisms? "It is good to be criticized," the pope said. "I welcome it, always. Life is full of misunderstandings and tensions. And when they are criticisms that lead to growth, I accept them, I respond. But the most difficult questions aren't asked by the religious, but by the young people. Young people put you in trouble, they do. Lunches with the kids at the World Youth Days or on other occasions, these situations can be tough. Young people are brash and sincere, and they ask the hardest things. Now go ahead, ask your questions."

Holy Father, we have seen your ability to speak to young people and to inspire them for the cause of the Gospel. We also know of your commitment to bring young people closer to the church. It is why you've called for the next meeting of the Synod of Bishops [in October 2018] to focus on the topic of young people, faith, and vocational discernment. What reasons led you to this choice? What guidance does it offer us in our efforts to reach out to young people today?

At the end of the last meeting of the synod, each participant was invited to offer three suggestions for the topic to be addressed by the next one. Then the episcopal conferences were consulted. Some strong common themes emerged, such as young people, priestly formation, interreligious dialogue, and peace. There was a good discussion about this at the first post-synodal council. I was there. I always go to those, but I don't speak. For me it is important to really listen. It is important that I listen, but I let them work freely. In this way

I understand how the problems emerge, what the proposals and the problems are, and how they are addressed.

They chose young people. But some emphasized the importance of priestly formation. Personally, I have the issue of discernment very much at heart. I have recommended it several times to the Jesuits, in Poland and then again to the general congregation.[1] Discernment brings together the question of the formation of young people and life—of all young people but in particular, even more so, of seminarians and future shepherds. Because formation and accompaniment to the priesthood needs discernment.

It is one of the biggest problems we have at the moment in priestly formation. In formation, we are used to formulas, everything black and white, but not the grays of life. And what matters is life, not formulas. We must grow in discernment. The logic of black and white can lead to casuistic abstraction. But discernment is about stepping forward into the grays of life according to God's will. And God's will is sought according to the true doctrine of the Gospel, not in the "fixedness" of an abstract doctrine. Thinking about the formation of young people and the formation of seminarians, I decided on the final theme as it was expressed: "Young People, Faith, and Vocational Discernment."

The church must accompany young people on their journey toward maturity, and only with discernment and not with abstractions can young people discover the purpose of their lives and live a life truly open to God and to the world. So I chose this theme to introduce discernment more emphatically into the life of the church. The other day we had the second meeting of the post-synodal council. There was a good discussion on this subject. They have prepared the first draft of the *Lineamenta*, which will be sent to the episcopal conferences next. Religious also worked on it. A well-prepared draft has emerged.

But this is the key point: discernment, which is always dynamic, like life. Static things don't work. Especially with young people. When I was young, the fashion was to have meetings. Static things like meetings are no good today. You have to work with young people by doing things, doing mission work, social work, going every week to feed the homeless. Young people find the Lord in action. Then, after the action, there must be reflection. But reflection by itself doesn't help—it's ideas, just ideas.

So two words: *listening* and *action*. This is important. Not only to form young people to listen, but above all to listen to them, to the young people themselves. This is a very important first task of the church: listening to young people. And in the preparation for the synod meeting, the presence of religious is truly important because the religious do a lot of work with young people.

What do you ask of religious life in preparing for the synod? What hopes do you have for the next synod on young people, in light of the diminishing strength of religious life in the West?

Of course, it's true that the strength of religious life in the West is decreasing. This certainly is related to demographics. But it is also true that sometimes the ministry of vocations does not respond to the expectations of young people. The next synod will provide us with some ideas. The diminishment of religious life in the West worries me.

But another thing also worries me: the rise of some new religious institutes that raise some concerns. I'm not saying that there should be no new religious institutes. Of course not. But in some cases I wonder what is happening today. Some of them seem like a great novelty, they seem to express enormous apostolic strength, they draw many people, and then…they fail. Sometimes it even turns out that there were scandalous things going on in the background.

There are some small, new foundations that are really good and that are serious. I see that behind these good foundations there are sometimes also groups of bishops who accompany and support their growth. But there are others that arise not from a charism of the Holy Spirit, but from human charisma, from a charismatic person who attracts followers through his appealing human qualities. Some are what I would call "restorationist"—they seem to offer security but in fact offer only rigidity. When they tell me that there is a new institute that is attracting so many vocations, I confess that I worry. The Spirit does not work with the logic of human success; it has another way. But they tell me: there are many young people who are fully committed, who pray a lot, who are very faithful. And I say to myself, "Very well. We'll see if it is of the Lord."

And some are Pelagian—they want to return to asceticism, they do penances, they seem like soldiers ready to do anything to defend the faith and good morals…and then the scandal of the founder or foundress emerges. We don't know, do we?

The style of Jesus is different. The Holy Spirit made noise on the day of Pentecost. That was at the beginning. But usually he doesn't make a lot of noise; he carries the cross. The Holy Spirit is not a triumphalist. God's style is the cross that is carried forward until the Lord says "enough." Triumphalism does not go well with consecrated life.

So don't put your hope in the big and sudden flowering of these institutes. Instead, seek the humble path of Jesus, that of evangelical witness. Benedict XVI told us very well: the church does not grow by proselytism, but by attraction.

Why did you choose the three Marian themes for the next three annual World Youth Days that will culminate in the international celebration of World Youth Day in Panama [in 2019]?

The Marian themes for the next three World Youth Days weren't chosen by me. From Latin America they asked for that—a strong Marian presence. It is true that Latin America is very Marian, and it seemed like a very good thing to me. I hadn't received any other proposals, and I was happy with that.

But the *true* Madonna! Not Our Lady who is the head of a post office, sending a different letter every day, saying, "My children, do this," and then the next day, "Do this." No, that's not her. The true Madonna is the one who instills Jesus in our hearts, the one who is Mother. This trend of a superstar Madonna, a protagonist who puts herself at the center, isn't Catholic.

Holy Father, your mission in the church is not easy. Despite the challenges, tensions, and oppositions, you offer us the example of a serene man, a man of peace. What is the source of your serenity? Where does this trust that inspires you—and that can also help sustain our own mission—come from? What advice would you offer us who are called to be religious guides, to help us carry out our task responsibly and peacefully?

What is the source of my serenity? No, I don't take sedatives! The Italians offer a good bit of advice: to live in peace, one has to have a healthy indifference. I'm willing to say this is a completely new experience for me. I admit that in Buenos Aires, I was more anxious. I felt more tense and worried. In short, I was not like I am now. I had a very particular experience of profound peace from the moment I was elected. And it hasn't left me since then. I live in peace. I can't explain it.

They tell me that for the conclave, the betting in London put me at number forty-two or forty-six. I didn't foresee it at all. I had my homily ready for Holy Thursday [in Buenos Aires].[2] The newspapers were saying that I was a "kingmaker," but not the pope. At the time of the election, I simply said, "Lord, let's go forward!" I felt peace, and that peace has not gone away.

In the [conclave's] general congregations, there was talk of the Vatican's problems, talk of reform. Everyone wanted it. There is corruption at the Vatican. But I am at peace. If there is a problem, I write a note to Saint Joseph and put it under a statue that I have in my room. It is a statue of Saint Joseph sleeping. And now he sleeps upon a mattress of notes! This is why I sleep well—it's a grace of God. I always sleep six hours.

And I pray. I pray in my way. I like the breviary so much, and I never leave it. Mass every day. The rosary. When I pray, I always use the Bible. And my peace grows. I don't know if this is the secret. My peace is a gift from the Lord. May it never leave me!

I believe that each one must find the root of the call that the Lord offers him. After all, losing our peace doesn't help us suffer. Superiors must learn how to suffer, but to suffer like a father. And also to suffer with great humility. By traveling this path, one goes from the cross to peace. But never wash your hands of problems! Yes, in the church there are Pontius Pilates who wash their hands of things so they can rest easy. But a superior who washes his hands of things isn't a father and doesn't help.

Holy Father, you have often commented that what distinguishes religious life is prophecy. We have discussed at length what it means to be radical in prophecy. What are the "comfort zones" that we are called to leave behind? You spoke to the sisters about a "prophetic and credible asceticism." How do you understand this in the context of a "culture of mercy"? How can consecrated life contribute to this culture?

Be radical in prophecy. To me, this means so much. I will take Joel 2 as an "icon" of this. It often comes to mind, and I know it comes from God. It says, "Your sons and daughters shall prophesy, your old men will dream dreams" [Joel 2:28]. This verse is the spirituality of the generations in a nutshell. Being radical in prophecy is the famous *sine glossa*, the rule *sine glossa*, the Gospel *sine glossa*. That is, without sedatives! The Gospel needs to be taken without sedatives, as it was for our founders.

We must find the radicality of prophecy in our founders. They remind us that we are called to leave our comfort zones and security, to leave all that is of the world, in our way of life, but also in forging new ways for our communities. New paths must be sought in the foundational charism and the initial prophecy. We must recognize, personally and as a community, the ways of our own worldliness.

Even the ascetic can be worldly. But instead he must be prophetic. When I entered the Jesuit novitiate, they gave me the hairshirt. The hairshirt is fine, but be careful: it's not about showing myself how good and strong I am. True ascesis must make me freer. I believe fasting is something that remains relevant—but how do I fast? By simply not eating? Little Saint Teresa had another way: she never said what she liked to eat. She didn't complain and took everything they gave her. Small, daily asceticism is a constant mortification.

I am reminded of a phrase from Saint Ignatius that helps us to be freer and happier. He said mortification in all things possible helps us follow the Lord. If something helps you, do it, even the hairshirt! But only if it helps you be freer, not because you need it to show yourself how strong you are.

What does community life involve? What is the role of a superior in nurturing its prophecy? What contribution can religious make to contribute to the renewal of the structures and mentalities of the church?

Community life. Some saints have called it a continuous penance. There are communities where people constantly nag and criticize each other! If there is no mercy in the community, that's a problem. For religious, the capacity to forgive often starts within the community. And this is prophetic. It always begins with listening—everyone needs to feel heard. It also takes listening and persuasion on the part of the superior. If all the superior ever does is criticize, this gets in the way of nurturing the radical prophecy of religious life. I am convinced that religious have an advantage in contributing to the renewal of the structures and mentality of the church.

In the presbyteral councils of the dioceses, religious help on the journey. And they shouldn't be afraid to speak up. A worldly and princely climate develops in the structures of the church, and religious can contribute to destroying this nefarious climate. One doesn't have to be a cardinal to begin thinking he's a prince! It's enough to be clerical. This is the worst thing about the organization of the church. Religious can offer the witness of humbler fraternity. They bear the witness of an upside-down iceberg, where the tip, the top of it, is at the bottom.

Holy Father, we have hopes that under your leadership better relations will develop between the consecrated life and particular churches. What does it mean for us to fully express our charisms within the particular churches and to address the difficulties that sometimes arise in our relations with bishops and diocesan clergy? How do you understand the realization of the dialogue between religious life and the bishops, in our collaboration with the local church?

For some time there has been a desire to review the guidelines for relations between bishops and religious orders that were established in 1978 by the Congregation for Religious and the Congregation for Bishops in the document *Mutuae Relationes*. This was mentioned during the synod of 1994. That document is addressed to a certain time and is no longer very relevant. The time is ripe for change.

It is important that religious feel like they are fully a part of the diocesan church. Fully. Sometimes there are misunderstandings that damage unity, and then we need to identify the problems.

Religious need to be part of the governing structures of the local church—administrative councils, presbyteral councils, and so on. In Buenos Aires, the religious elected their representatives to the presbyteral council. The work must be shared within the diocesan structures. Religious should be part of the governing structures of the diocese. In isolation, we do not help each other. There is room for a lot of growth in this area. This also helps the bishop to avoid the temptation of becoming a little prince.

But spirituality too must be shared, and religious are the bearers of strong spiritual traditions. In some dioceses, the diocesan priests gather in groups for spirituality that is Franciscan, Carmelite, and so on. But the very style of life can be shared. Some diocesan priests wonder why they can't live together so they're not so alone, why they can't live a more communal life. This desire comes, for example, when you have the good witness of a parish run by a community of religious. There is a level of radical collaboration because it is spiritual, from the soul. And the clergy and religious of a diocese being spiritually close helps avoid potential misunderstandings. You can study and think through many things. That includes the question of the duration of a priest's service at a parish, which seems short to me; the parish priests are changed too easily.

I won't deny that there are many other problems at a third level, which is economic management. When the wallet is involved, there are problems. I'm thinking of the issue of the misuse of assets. We have to be very cautious about assets. Poverty is a constant in the life of the church, both in its observance and its failure to be observed. The consequences are always heavy.

Holy Father, like the church in general, religious orders are also committed to addressing the problem of sexual abuse of minors and financial abuse with transparency and determination. These realities are counterwitnesses. They cause scandal. And they also have a negative impact on both vocations and the help of benefactors. What measures do you suggest to us to prevent such scandals in our congregations?

Perhaps there isn't enough time for a very detailed answer, and I rely on your wisdom. But regarding finances, let me say that the Lord really wants religious to be poor. When they are not, the Lord sends a treasurer who brings the order into bankruptcy! Sometimes religious congregations get the help of an administrator who is considered a "friend" and who then makes them fail. But a fundamental criterion for a treasurer is not to be personally attached to money. Once it happened that a nun who was the community's treasurer fainted, and one of the other sisters said to those who were helping her, "Pass a banknote under her nose and she'll recover quickly!" That makes us laugh, but also reflect. It is also important to check how the banks invest the money. It must never happen that there are investments in arms, for example. Never.

Regarding sexual abuse, it seems that out of every four people who abuse, two have been abused themselves. Abuse is sown into the future. It is devastating. Any time priests or religious are involved, the devil is in action, ruining the work of Jesus through the one who was supposed to proclaim Jesus. But let's be clear: this is a sickness. If we are not convinced that this is a sickness, the problem cannot be addressed well. Therefore, be careful not to receive candidates for religious life into formation without making sure of their adequate affective maturity. For example: never receive candidates into religious life or into a diocese who have been rejected by another seminary or another order without asking for very clear and detailed information on the reasons for their removal.

Holy Father, religious life is not an end in itself; it exists for its mission in the world. You have invited us to be a church that goes forth. In your view, is religious life throughout the world bringing about this conversion?

The church was born going forth. It was locked in the Upper Room, and then it went forth. And it has to stay out. It can't go back to closing itself in the Upper Room. Jesus wanted it this way. And "out" means what I call the peripheries, existential and social. The existential poor and the social poor draw the church out of itself.

Let us think of one form of poverty—the problem of migrants and refugees. More important than international agreements are the *lives* of those people! And it is precisely in the service of charity that it is also possible to find excellent ground for ecumenical dialogue: it is the poor who unite divided Christians! These are all open challenges for religious in a church that moves beyond itself.

Evangelii Gaudium wants to communicate this need to go forth. I would like us to return to that apostolic exhortation with reflection and prayer. It matured in the light of *Evangelii Nuntiandi* and the work done at Aparecida. It contains a broad ecclesial reflection.

And finally, let us always remember: mercy is God going forth. And God is always merciful. You go forth, too!

———

The meeting ended at around 1:00 p.m. with a few words of thanks and a long applause. Just before leaving the hall, the pope offered everyone these words: "Move forward with courage and without fear of making mistakes! The only one who never makes mistakes is the one who does nothing. We must move forward! Sometimes we will make mistakes, yes, but there is always God's mercy on our side." Before leaving, Francis greeted all those present once again, one by one.

NOTES

PREFACE

1. We should keep in mind that Francis speaks not only from the point of view of doctrine and tradition, but also from personal experience. He is, in fact, the first pope who is a member of a religious order since the Camaldolese monk Bartolomeo Alberto Cappellari was elected and became Gregory XVI in 1831.

2. *La Civiltà Cattolica* is a periodical published in Rome by the Jesuit order. Its contents are approved by the Vatican Secretary of State. Founded in 1850, it is one of the oldest Catholic periodicals in the world.

CHAPTER 1: A CONVERSATION WITH RELIGIOUS SUPERIORS, NOVEMBER 29, 2013

1. The assembly was held November 27–29, 2013, at the Pontifical Salesian University (known more commonly as the Salesianum) in Rome. It was a meeting structured around three principal addresses

that guided subsequent reflections. Fr. Janson Hervé, of the Little Brothers of Jesus, spoke about "the principles that help me to live this service of my brothers and how Pope Francis strengthens my hope." Br. Mauro Jöhri, Capuchin, explained "how Pope Francis is inspiring and challenging me in the service of leadership within my order." Finally, Fr. Hainz Kulüke, of the Society of the Divine Word, focused on "leadership within a missionary religious congregation in an international and intercultural context in the light of the example of Pope Francis."

2. Shortly after he completed his tenure as provincial of the Jesuits of Argentina, Jorge Mario Bergoglio published a collection of reflections he had given to confreres, *Meditaciones para religiosos* (San Miguel: Ediciones Diego De Torres, 1982). This book is illuminating in helping us to understand some key themes that Bergoglio would develop later, including as pope. The volume has been published in Italian as *Nel cuore di ogni padre: Alle radici della mia spiritualità* (Milan: Rizzoli, 2014).

3. Cf. Pope Benedict XVI, "Homily at Holy Mass for the Inauguration of the Fifth General Conference of the Bishops of Latin America and the Caribbean" (May 13, 2007). Available at http://www.vatican.va/content/benedict-xvi/en/homilies/2007/documents/hf_ben-xvi_hom_20070513_conference-brazil.html. Pope Francis has repeatedly referred to and echoed this concept of his predecessor. He did so, for example, in his homily at Mass in the chapel of the Santa Marta residence on October 1: "'The Church,' as

Benedict XVI has told us, 'grows by attraction, by witness. And when people, when peoples see this witness of humility, meekness, and docility, they feel the need' which the prophet Zecharaiah spoke of, saying: 'Let us go with you.' Faced with the witness of charity, people feel this need....Charity is simple: worshiping God and serving others." Available at http://www.vatican .va/content/francesco/en/cotidie/2013/documents/ papa-francesco-cotidie_20131001_humility-gospel .html. (The portions of this passage outside of the secondary quotation marks are the Vatican summary of the pope's words; full verbatim transcripts of the morning homilies are not available.) See also Pope Francis's October 4, 2013, address during his visit to the Cathedral of San Rufino in Assisi, and the apostolic exhortation *Evangelii Gaudium* 14.

4. See Pope Francis, apostolic exhortation *Evangelii Gaudium* (November 24, 2013): "Here our model is not the sphere, which is no greater than its parts, where every point is equidistant from the center, and there are no differences between them. Instead, it is the polyhedron, which reflects the convergence of all its parts, each of which preserves its distinctiveness" (no. 236). Available at http://www.vatican.va/content/ francesco/en/apost_exhortations/documents/papa -francesco_esortazione-ap_20131124_evangelii -gaudium.html.

5. Pope Francis also cited this letter of Fr. Arrupe in the 2013 *La Civiltà Cattolica* interview, calling it "brilliant." See Antonio Spadaro, SJ, "A Big Heart Open to God: An Interview with Pope Francis," *America*,

September 30, 2013. Available at https://www
.americamagazine.org/faith/2013/09/30/big-heart
-open-god-interview-pope-francis.

6. Spadaro, "A Big Heart Open to God."

7. This misunderstanding of the late-sixteenth/
early-seventeenth century was due to the fact that, in
their missionary work, the Jesuits tried to adapt the
proclamation of the Gospel to local cultures and reli-
gions. But some in the church were troubled by this
approach and opposed it, claiming that it led to a
contamination of the Christian message. The Jesuits'
prophetic approach was rejected at the time because it
went beyond the commonly accepted understanding
of the facts.

8. Fr. Segundo Llorente (1906–89) was a Spanish Jesuit who spent over forty years as a missionary
in Alaska. He was elected without campaigning to be
representative for the state to the United States Congress, and he is considered to be a cofounder of the
state. After his death, he was buried in a Native American cemetery in De Smet, Idaho. When he arrived in
Akulurak at the age of twenty-nine, his first challenges
included not only learning the Eskimo language but
talking about God to people with a way of thinking
that was radically different from that of Europe. He
wrote twelve books on his missionary experience.

9. Pope Francis, "Address to the Leadership of
the Episcopal Conferences of Latin America during
the General Coordination Meeting" (July 28, 2013),
no. 4.3. Available at http://www.vatican.va/content/

:n/speeches/2013/july/documents/papa
20130728_gmg-celam-rio.html.

aint John (Jan) Berchmans (1599–1621)
ian Jesuit canonized by Pope Leo XIII in
1ade his first religious profession as a Jesuit
d the following year he moved to Rome to
1is philosophical studies at the Roman Col-
e, falling ill, he died after only two years,
: 13, 1621. Faithful to his favorite mottos—
agis ("Whatever you are doing, do it well")
imi facere minima ("Make the most of the
1e performed ordinary things in an extraordinary way and became known as the saint of common life.

11. Pope Francis, *Evangelii Gaudium* 226.

12. Pope Francis, *Evangelii Gaudium* 227.

13. Cf. Jorge Mario Bergoglio/Pope Francis, *È l'amore che apre gli occhi* (Milan: Rizzoli, 2013), 46.

14. *Guarda a la Iglesia de quien fue figura / la inmaculada y maternal María; / guárdala intacta, firme y con ternura / de eucaristía* ("Guard the church of which / the immaculate and maternal Mary was the figure / keep it intact, firm, and with the tenderness / of the Eucharist").

15. See Pope Francis, "Address to the Community of Writers of *La Civiltà Cattolica*" (June 14, 2013). Available at http://www.vatican.va/content/francesco/en/speeches/2013/june/documents/papa-francesco_20130614_la-civilta-cattolica.html.

16. When he was the archbishop of Buenos Aires, Cardinal Bergoglio addressed issues related

to education frequently in speeches. See Jorge Mario Bergoglio/Pope Francis, *Education for Choosing Life: Proposals for Difficult Times* (San Francisco: Ignatius, 2014).

CHAPTER 2: POPE FRANCIS'S EIGHT CHALLENGES FOR CONSECRATED LIFE

1. Pope Francis, *Apostolic Letter to All Consecrated People on the Occasion of the Year of Consecrated Life* (November 21, 2014). Available at http://www.vatican.va/content/francesco/en/apost_letters/documents/papa-francesco_lettera-ap_20141121_lettera-consacrati.html.

2. Bishop Bergoglio's intervention is available in Giuseppe Ferraro, ed., *Il Sinodo dei Vescovi: Nona Assemblea Generale Ordinaria (2–30 ottobre 1994)* (Rome: La Civiltà Cattolica, 1998), 278.

3. Ferraro, *Il Sinodo dei Vescovi*, 278.

4. Pope John Paul II, "Address to the Superiors General of Men's Religious Orders" (November 24, 1978). Available at http://www.vatican.va/content/john-paul-ii/en/speeches/1978/documents/hf_jp-ii_spe_19781124_superiori-generali.html.

5. Ferraro, *Il Sinodo dei Vescovi*, 278.

6. Pope Francis, "Homily on the Occasion of the Feast of Saint Ignatius" (July 31, 2013).

7. Pope Francis, "Address to the Communion and Liberation Movement" (March 7, 2015). Available at http://www.vatican.va/content/francesco/en/speeches/2015/march/documents/papa-francesco_20150307_comunione-liberazione.html.

8. See above, p. 3.

9. See above, p. 4.

10. Pope Francis, "Holy Mass on the Liturgical Memorial of the Most Holy Name of Jesus" (January 3, 2014). Available at http://www.vatican.va/content/francesco/en/homilies/2014/documents/papa-francesco_20140103_omelia-santissimo-nome-gesu.html.

11. Antonio Spadaro, SJ, "A Big Heart Open to God: An Interview with Pope Francis," *America*, September 30, 2013. Available at https://www.americamagazine.org/faith/2013/09/30/big-heart-open-god-interview-pope-francis.

12. Pope Francis, "Homily at Holy Mass for the Beginning of the General Chapter of the Order of Saint Augustine" (August 28, 2013). Available at http://www.vatican.va/content/francesco/en/homilies/2013/documents/papa-francesco_20130828_capitolo-sant-agostino.html.

13. Pope Francis, *Apostolic Letter to All Consecrated People*, I.1.

14. Pope Francis, *Nel cuore di ogni padre: Alle radici della mia spiritualità* (Milan: Rizzoli, 2014).

15. Pope Francis, *Nel cuore di ogni padre*, 280.

16. Spadaro, "A Big Heart Open to God."

17. Pope Francis, "Holy Mass on the Liturgical Memorial of the Most Holy Name of Jesus," quoting Saint Peter Faber's *Memorial* 68.

18. Pope Francis, *Apostolic Letter to All Consecrated People*, II.4.

19. Pope Francis, *Nel cuore di ogni padre*, 259.

20. Pope Francis, *Evangelii Gaudium* 155.

21. See above, p. 12.

22. Pope Francis, "Homily for the Ordinary Public Consistory for the Creation of New Cardinals" (February 14, 2015). Available at http://www.vatican.va/content/francesco/en/homilies/2015/documents/papa-francesco_20150214_omelia-concistoro-nuovi-cardinali.html.

23. Pope Francis, *Nel cuore di ogni padre*, 158.

24. As we have noted above, the question of the relationship between the religious and the local church with its bishop emerged clearly in the pope's conversation with the superiors general, and he expressed interest in a revision of the 1978 document on this topic, *Mutuae Relationes*.

25. Pope Francis, *Nel cuore di ogni padre*, 38.

26. Pope Francis, *Nel cuore di ogni padre*, 274.

27. See above, p. 4.

28. See above, p. 7. Cf. Pope John Paul II, post-synodal apostolic exhortation *Vita Consecrata* (1996): "Look to the future, where the Spirit is sending you in order to do even greater things" (no. 110). Regarding the temptation to play at being prophets and the invitation not to reduce religious life to a light, disembodied, and gnostic "caricature," see also Pope Francis, "Homily for the Feast of the Presentation of the Lord, XIX World Day of Consecrated Life" (February 2, 2015). Available at http://www.vatican.va/content/francesco/en/homilies/2015/documents/papa-francesco_20150202_omelia-vita-consacrata.html.

29. Spadaro, "A Big Heart Open to God."

30. Yves Congar, *True and False Reform in the Church*, trans. Paul Philibert (Collegeville, MN: Liturgical Press, 2010), 183.

31. Pope Francis, *Apostolic Letter to All Consecrated People*, I.1.

32. See above, p. 8.

33. See above, p. 9.

34. Pope Francis, "Address to the Communion and Liberation Movement."

35. Pope Francis, *Apostolic Letter to All Consecrated People*, I.1.

36. Spadaro, "A Big Heart Open to God."

37. Pope Francis, *Nel cuore di ogni padre*, 108.

38. Pope Francis, *Nel cuore di ogni padre*, 15.

39. Pope Francis, *Nel cuore di ogni padre*, 133–34.

40. Pope Francis, *Nel cuore di ogni padre*, 64.

41. Pope Francis, *Nel cuore di ogni padre*, 55.

42. Pope Francis, *Nel cuore di ogni padre*, 45.

43. See Pope Francis, *Nel cuore di ogni padre*, 45–46.

44. Pope Francis, *Apostolic Letter to All Consecrated People*, II.2.

45. See above, p. 15.

46. Ferraro, *Il Sinodo dei Vescovi*, 278.

47. Pope Francis, *Apostolic Letter to All Consecrated People*, II.2.

48. Pope Francis, "Homily at Holy Mass for the Beginning of the General Chapter of the Order of Saint Augustine."

49. See above, p. 16.

50. See above, p. 17.

51. Pope Francis, *Apostolic Letter to All Consecrated People*, I.1; also III.1.

52. See above, p. 18.

53. See above, p. 19.

54. See above, p. 21.

55. Pope Francis, "Address to the Community of Writers of *La Civiltà Cattolica*"; quoting Pope Benedict XVI (who was quoting Pope Paul VI), "Address to the Fathers of the General Congregation of the Society of Jesus" (February 21, 2008).

56. Cf. Spadaro, "A Big Heart Open to God."

57. Pope Francis, "Address to Participants in the Ecclesial Convention of the Diocese of Rome" (June 17, 2013). Available at http://www.vatican.va/content/francesco/en/speeches/2013/june/documents/papa-francesco_20130617_convegno-diocesano-roma.html.

58. See above, p. 22.

59. See above, p. 23.

60. See above, p. 23.

61. Pope Francis, "Angelus" (December 7, 2014). Available at http://www.vatican.va/content/francesco/en/angelus/2014/documents/papa-francesco_angelus_20141207.html.

62. Pope Francis, "Address at the Celebration of Vespers with Priests, Men and Women Religious, Seminarians, and Various Lay Movements" (September 21, 2014). Available at http://www.vatican.va/content/francesco/en/speeches/2014/september/documents/papa-francesco_20140921_albania-celebrazione-vespri.html.

63. Antonio Spadaro, "Il viaggio de Papa Francesco nella Repubblica di Corea. Custodia, Empatia, Consolazione," *La Civiltà Cattolica* 3 (2014): 403–18.

64. Pope Francis, "Angelus" (December 7, 2014).

65. See above, p. 4.

66. Pope Francis, *Evangelii Gaudium* 155; cf. *Apostolic Letter to All Consecrated People*, II.3.

CHAPTER 3: "THE GOSPEL WITHOUT SEDATIVES"

1. See Antonio Spadaro, "'Today the Church Needs to Grow in Discernment': Pope Francis Meets with Polish Jesuits," *La Civiltà Cattolica* English ed., December 11, 2018, available at https://www.lacivilta cattolica.com/today-the-church-needs-to-grow-in -discernment-pope-francis-meets-with-polish -jesuits/; "'Avere coraggio e audacia profetica': Dialogo di papa Francesco con i gesuiti riuniti nella 36a Congregazione Generale," *La Civiltà Cattolica*, December 10, 2016, available at https://www.laciviltacattolica.it/ articolo/avere-coraggio-e-audacia-profetica-dialogo -di-papa-francesco-con-i-gesuiti-riuniti-nella-36a -congregazione-generale/ (no English ed. available).

2. This homily is found in Pope Francis, *Nei tuoi occhi è la mia parola: Omelie e discorsi di Buenos Aires 1999–2013* (Milan: Rizzoli, 2016), 952–54.